# North Wales
## PANORAMAS

SIMON KIRWAN

MYRIAD

LONDON

# CONTENTS

# NORTH SNOWDONIA

North Snowdonia, with the dominating Snowdon range at its heart, provides a spectacular backdrop to the coastal scenery of all north-west Wales. Over half a million visitors a year come to the area to enjoy some of Britain's finest mountain scenery

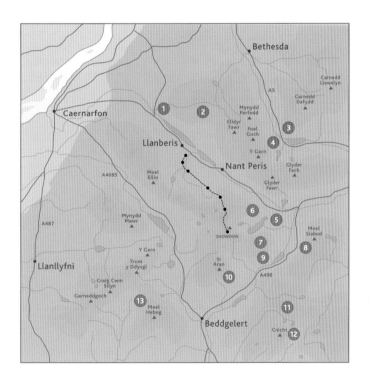

## OPPOSITE – LLYN LLYDAW

Nestling just below Snowdon, Llyn Llydaw is fed by the many streams running off the north-eastern slopes of the mountain. It is the Welsh claimant to be the home of the Lady of the Lake, famous from the Arthurian legend as the keeper of the sword Excalibur – although at 1400ft (427m) it would have been an unlikely if spectacular resting place for the sword

LLYN PADARN

The beautiful Llyn Padarn stands at the entrance to the Llanberis Pass on the northern side of Snowdon. At the far end of the two-mile long lake with Snowdon looming in the background you can just see the tower of Dolbadarn Castle in which Llewelyn, prince of Gwynedd, imprisoned his brother Owain Goch for 22 long years in 1255. On the shore of Llyn Padarn (the former site of Dinorwig slate quarries which employed 3,000 men) is a country park with a slate museum, railway and wooded walks along the lake shore.

SNOWDON & LLANBERIS

This photograph looks across Llyn Padarn towards the dramatic Snowdon range with the town of Llanberis on the far shore. The Llanberis pass which starts just after the town and disappears to the left of the photograph separates the Snowdon range on its right from the Glyders. The top of Snowdon can just be seen poking out behind the largest peak on the left – Crib y Dydsgl.

PEN YR OLE WEN

Pen yr Ole Wen on the left of the photograph with Llyn Ogwen alongside has a classic pointed shape with rough craggy features which make it one of the most recognisable peaks in north Snowdonia. Climbers who tackle the mountain at the westernmost tip of Llyn Ogwen are faced with a relentless 45° climb to the summit. On the other side of the lake the 'shark fin' of Tryfan is just visible.

CWM IDWAL

The hanging valley of Cwm Idwal is a magnet for climbers and geologists. Close to the A5 south of Braichmelyn, glacial action has carved out a deep incision leaving a dark-coloured lake – Llyn Idwal – surrounded by a semi-circle of steep rocky slopes. Giant rock falls surround the base of the steepest rock walls making the whole area appear more like the surface of the moon than a north Wales' valley.

GLYDER FAWR

Glyder Fawr (3,278ft/999m) and its adjoining sister peak Glyder Fach (3,248ft/990m) are linked by a one mile (1600m) ridge. The Glyders lie directly north of Snowdon and from the rocky summits you can look down on Llyn Idwal, the Ogwen valley and, in good weather, enjoy uninterrupted views north across Anglesey to the Irish Sea.

LLYN LLYDAW

Snowdon is surrounded by a number of interconnected lakes which drain the area around the highest peaks. Here, at the upper end of Llyn Llydaw at the northern end of the lake next to the well-worn path to the summit known as the Miner's Track, is the inflow into Llyn Llydaw from Glaslyn, the first lake in the chain.

CRIB GOCH

Most visitors reach the summit of Snowdon using the mountain railway from Llanberis which terminates 66ft from the top. A much more daunting challenge, particularly in winter, is to approach the peak from the eastern flank of the mountain via the adjoining peak of Crib Goch and walk along the sharp ridge or arête (the 'Snowdon horseshoe' as it is often called) towards Snowdon. Snowdon and its ridge can be seen clearly towards the left of the photograph with Crib Goch dominating the view looming over Llyn Llydaw in the foreground.

SNOWDON

Even though the north and western sides of Snowdon look a great deal less formidable in winter than its precipitous eastern flank, the views are splendid whether you are walking or travelling on the Snowdon mountain railway. From the summit at 3560ft (1085m) you can look back down the mountain to the Lleyn peninsula and across Caernarfon Bay. This photograph is taken from a viewpoint close to the road on the Nant Gwynant pass.

NANT GWYNANT

Between Beddgelert and Pen-y-Gwryd on the south side of Snowdon lies Nant Gwynant, one of North Snowdonia's finest valleys, which contains two twin lakes – Llyn Dinas, named after the lakeside iron-age hill fort of Dinas Emrys and Llyn Gwynant, which many say is the most beautiful stretch of water in the country. As the A498 climbs the shoulder of the Nant Gwynant pass there are panoramic views of Snowdon and its neighbouring peaks.

LLYN DINAS

Between Beddgelert and Plas Gwynant close to the hill fort of Dinas Emrys lies the mysterious and beautiful Llyn Dinas, seen here from the west side of the lake. It is said to have been the site of an ancient battle between Owein, one of King Arthur's greatest warriors and a giant. It is here also that the treacherous King Vortigern is reputed to have hidden the throne of the British kingdom behind a stone.

CNICHT SUMMIT

Its steep rocky faces and pyramid-shaped peak have earned Cnicht the nickname of the 'Welsh Matterhorn', but at 2260ft (689m) it's a dwarf compared to its alpine cousin. Set above the village of Croesor, the nearby valley was once alive with the hum and activity of slate quarrying but is now a quiet, beautiful backwater. From the summit you can enjoy the view inland towards the mountains of southern Snowdonia and to the south-west dramatic views across the wide expanses of the estuary towards Porthmadog and Tremadog Bay.

LLYN CWM-CORSIOG

Despite its natural appearance, Llyn Cwm-corsiog is an artificial lake created in 1899 to supply water to the remote slate mining quarry at Rhosydd, two miles west of Blaenau Ffestiniog. The lake is approximately 8 acres in size and was one of 12 lakes dotted around this area which were dammed to supply the quarry with water. Ironically, the water was mainly used to drive huge water pumps designed to prevent water flooding the mine workings.

NANTLLE RIDGE

The Nantlle ridge is part of a range of mountains stretching from the Bedgellert Forest in the east to the village of Pant Glas. Here the ridge is seen from the summit of Moel Hebog a few miles to the south. The range has 11 peaks over 1960ft (600m), seven of which are part of the ridge.

# NORTH-WEST COAST

Stretching from Prestatyn to the Lleyn peninsula, the north-west coast takes in an array of scenic beauty from tiny fishing villages on the north Anglesey coast such as Moelfre to the dramatic fortified towns of Conwy and Caernarfon

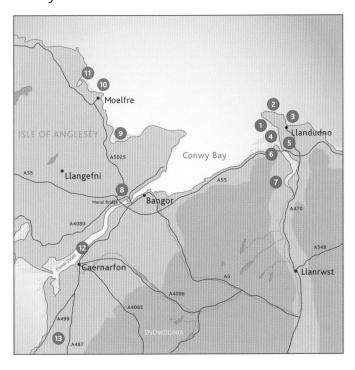

OPPOSITE – MENAI BRIDGE

Thomas Telford's masterpiece the Menai Bridge, linking the north Wales mainland with the Isle of Anglesey, was opened in 1826. Until then, Anglesey could only be reached by a hazardous ferry journey across the straits

GREAT ORME

Situated to the west of the Victorian resort town of Llandudno is Great Orme, a rocky peninsula which forms almost a separate island sticking out into the sea. The name Orme comes from the Norse and means 'great worm' or 'sea serpent', a very apt description for this unusual geological feature, particularly if, like the Vikings, you first sighted this formidable headland from the sea.

GREAT ORME SUMMIT

The summit of Great Orme can be reached by car, on foot or by using Britain's only remaining cable-operated street tramway which first began service here in 1902. To the west are magnificent views of Snowdonia and to the east the Little Orme – sister of the Great Orme which marks the far end of this rocky promontory.

LLANDUDNO PIER

Opened in 1878, Llandudno's magnificent pier is 2295ft (695m) long and is unusual in that it has a 45° turn roughly one-third of the way along its length. It has a 60ft (18m) wooden promenade with beautiful wrought-iron balustrades and four pairs of elegant kiosks along its length. At the end of the promenade are three further octagonal kiosks with a T-shaped pier head.

DEGANWY BEACH

From the beach front at Deganwy on the eastern mouth of the river Conwy you can enjoy eye-catching views looking west across the wide estuary which forms the mouth of the river Conwy. On the far bank high headlands marking the extreme northerly tip of Snowdonia drop down into the sea. The nearest hill is Conwy mountain.

CONWY

The dark-stoned fortress of Conwy Castle dominates the Conwy Estuary. Construction work began in 1283 (the same year as Caernarfon Castle) as part of an 'iron ring' of fortresses designed to subdue the local population. Unlike Caernarfon, Conwy Castle was not built with concentric walls – such was the strength of its site on a rocky promontory that a series of soaring curtain walls and eight huge round towers were considered strong enough to repel even the most determined attackers.

CONWY ESTUARY

The long estuary of the river Conwy provides a wide and safe expanse of water which is ideal for pleasure craft. This view downstream of Conwy from Conwy mountain is looking directly across the water to Llandudno Junction. Further left is the pretty seaside town of Deganwy which lies close to the mouth of the river.

GLAN CONWY

The vale of Conwy extends almost 30 miles (50km) inland and provides a peaceful and beautiful haven away from the busy coastal towns close to the mouth of the river. This section of the vale just south of the village of Glan Conwy shows how wide the river is despite the fact that we are almost 5 miles (8km) from the sea.

MENAI BRIDGE

One of the most famous suspension bridges in the world was completed over the Menai Straits in 1826. It utilised a remarkable new material at the time – wrought iron – from which the main links of the bridge were constructed. Critics said the span of 579ft (1900m) could never be bridged without supports but its architect, Thomas Telford, proved them wrong and built an elegant structure which has almost become an icon for this part of north Wales.

RED WHARF BAY

The wide sandy estuary of Red Wharf Bay is a haven for birdwatchers and those in search of an old-fashioned family seaside resort. The whitewashed houses which dot the edges of the bay add to the area's scenic charm.

MOELFRE

Moelfre on the north coast of Anglesey is an idyllic seaside resort with a picturesque beach, magnificent views towards Snowdonia and a centuries-old history of fishing and seafaring. The seafront is an excellent vantage point for spotting ocean-going and coastal vessels heading to and from Merseyside.

BULL BAY

Bull Bay (Porth Llechog) stands on a pretty headland just north of Amlwch on Anglesey's rocky north coast. Despite its idyllic appearance, this area is dangerous for both pleasure boats and for large cargo vessels approaching the port of Liverpool and the nearby lifeboat is kept busy throughout the year. From the clifftop walks between Bull Bay and Cemaes Bay you can enjoy the view across the Irish Sea and, on a clear day, see the Isle of Man, Cheshire and Merseyside.

CAERNARFON

When Caernarfon Castle was first constructed under the orders of Edward 1 in 1283 the building was intended to be a mighty fortress encompassing a military stronghold, seat of government and a royal palace. Viewed from a low vantage point on the edge of the harbour, the scale and dominating presence of Caernarfon make clear the original builder's intentions despite the passage of seven centuries. The castle is now a World Heritage Site.

LLEYN PENINSULA

The Lleyn peninsula (pronounced to rhyme with 'keen') contains the resorts of Abersoch and Pwllheli but most of the peninsula is a quiet place with charming little fishing villages and whitewashed farms. Here a magnificent sunset is captured looking along the southern coast of the peninsula from a point close to Harlech.

# SOUTH SNOWDONIA

Southern Snowdonia may not have the drama of the high peaks of the Snowdon range but it is packed with mountain scenery and beautiful green valleys – all without the crowds who flock further north

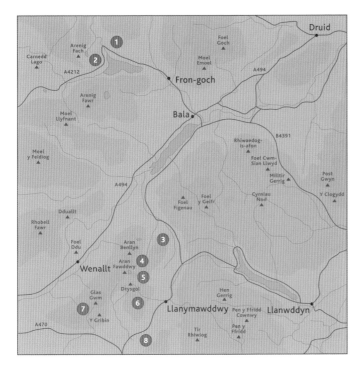

OPPOSITE – CWM CYWARCH
One of the dramatic crags of Cwm Cywarch – a west Wales magnet for any serious rock climber in the Aran mountains

LLYN CELYN AND MYNYDD NODOL

Llyn Celyn is south of the A4212 road from Bala to Trawsfynydd and was set up as a reservoir in 1965 to supply the city of Liverpool. Across the water, rising steeply from the surrounding countryside, is Mynydd Nodol (1768ft/539m).

LLYN CELYN

The peaceful waters of Llyn Celyn encircled by the photogenic Arenig mountains attract many visitors but the reservoir is dogged by controversy even to this day. Despite vigorous local opposition, the Tryweryn valley was flooded in 1965 and more than 12 farms were destroyed along with the village of Capel Celyn, its school, post office, chapel and cemetery.

CWM CYNLLWYD

High mountain ranges are more difficult to gain access to in southern Snowdonia compared to the north. But by road you can reach the northern end of the Arans by turning off the B4403 which runs along the east side of Bala Lake onto the smaller road leading to Tynant and Llanymawddwy. All along the south side of this road you will be rewarded by outstanding views of Aran Benllyn (2900ft/884m), Dyrysgol (2400ft/731m) and Aran Fawddwy.

ARAN FAWDDWY SUMMIT

The rounded summit of Aran Fawddwy looks barren but quite benign from this vantage point but the view hides Aran Fawddwy's dramatic 2.5mile (4km) long ridge with a 1000ft (300m) drop to Creiglyn Dyfi below. The view along the ridge to Aran Benllyn is superb with Bala Lake (Llyn Tegid) as a backdrop.

ARAN FAWDDWY

To the south of Bala Lake (Llyn Tegid) are the Arans, a range of mountains beloved of walkers and climbers who enjoy the great outdoors but want to get away from the more crowded slopes of the Snowdon range to the north. The Arans' best-known peak, and the highest in south Snowdonia at 2976ft (905m), is Aran Fawddwy. This craggy mountain overlooks the small lake or tarn of Creiglyn Dyfi which lies in a hollow beneath its steep cliff face.

CWM CYWARCH

This beautiful valley set in the Aran Mountains close to Dinas Mawddwy is a magnet for visitors who enjoy wide open landscapes. It offers both gentle walks to more strenuous rock-climbing for the experts. This photograph was taken from the gorge north of Glasgwm.

CWM CYWARCH CRAGS

The craggy cliffs of Cywarch at the head of the valley are a favourite with climbers. The vast cliff face offers dozens of different routes and is particularly challenging in winter. On the ridge to the right is a memorial cairn to a member of an RAF mountain rescue team who was killed by lightning in 1960.

AFON DYFI VALLEY

The main Dyfi valley runs alongside the A489 north-east of Machynlleth and is accepted as the traditional divide between north and south Wales where the rugged mountains of south Snowdonia meet the smooth rounded hills of mid Wales. The beautiful river rises close to Aberdyfi and makes its way to the sea near Borth, a distance of 108 miles (172km).

# WEST WALES

The western side of north Wales is a favourite both with lovers of coastal scenery and mountains. The area contains two dramatic inland estuaries plus mountains and lakeland scenery to match any in Britain

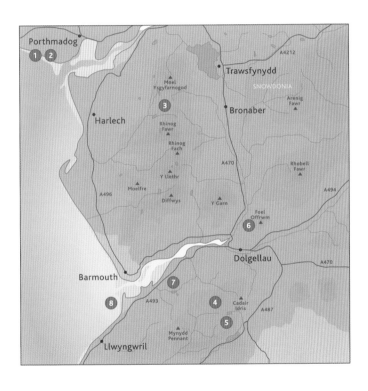

OPPOSITE – CREGENNEN LAKES
The peaceful waters of Cregennen Lakes – two beautiful stretches of water with scenic vistas on the southern side of the Mawddach estuary

PORTHMADOG

One of Porthmadog's greatest attractions is its position on the wide estuary where the river meets Tremadog Bay. If you head for Borth Y Gest, a small village less than a mile down river from the town, it is possible to walk the coastal footpath and enjoy spectacular views of the river, mud flats and the mountains.

MOEL Y GEST

The rounded granite peak of Moel Y Gest dominates the western approach to Porthmadog. Although the mountain is not particularly high at 859ft (262m) its exposed position gives tremendous views from the summit up and down the coast and inland to the estuary.

CWM BYCHAN

The Rhinog mountains lie to the west of the village of Llanbedr. A favourite route to approach them is via the lake at Llyn Cwm Bychan and then on to the farm at the top of the valley seen here in the photograph. A carefully laid series of flat stones, known as the Roman Steps, give you an easy walk up on to the higher ground. The peak on the right is Clip which offers a picturesque route to the summits of both Rhinog Fawr and Rhinog Fach.

CADAIR IDRIS

Cadair Idris – the chair of Idris, a giant of Welsh mythology – marks the southern-most limits of Snowdonia's mountains. At 2929ft (893m) it is a few metres lower than South Snowdonia's highest mountain, Aran Fawddwy, but Cadair's open aspect offers the visitor far better views. From the summit at Pen Y Gadair ('top of the chair') you can usually see the entire west Wales coastline and look towards the Snowdon range to the north.

LLYN CAU

Llyn Cau is in an almost perfect situation for a high mountain lake: dwarfed by the towering cliffs of Craig Cau on the south-east face of Pen Y Gadair. But every visitor to this location detects an almost sinister air in the impenetrable dark waters. Local legend has it that a night spent close to the lake will either make you a poet or a madman. Myth and superstition perhaps but it is probably best to head home before nightfall just in case!

LLYN CYNWCH

Llyn Cynwch lies east of the village of Nannau, north of Dolgellau. Its picturesque setting tucked away amongst wooded hillsides and with views of Cadair Idris to the south make it a favourite with visitors who want to get off the beaten track. The lake is close to the well-known Precipice Walk, a two-mile route which gives incomparable views of the estuary and Llyn Cynwch.

CREGENNEN LAKES

Tucked away but easily accessible by car are the two Cregennen lakes which are set on a plateau on the south side of the side of the Mawddach Estuary. All around the lakes are impressive hillocks similar to the one shown here which are ideal vantage points to take in the panoramic views south to Barmouth and the sea and inland to the foothills of Cadair Idris.

MAWDDACH ESTUARY

The estuary of the Mawddach is 9 miles (15km) long and joins the sea south of Barmouth. This photograph is taken close to Fairbourne on the opposite side of the estuary to Barmouth. The picturesque Mawddach Trail – built on the track of a disused railway – carries walkers and cyclists along the banks of the estuary where two large bird reserves are situated.

## MOEL FAMAU

Set amongst the lush green pastures of the Vale of Clwyd, Moel Famau is a country park of 2,000 acres named after the highest mountain in the area. Seen here in early winter, a sprinkling of snow makes the wooded slopes of Moel Famau (1818ft/554m) stand out in stark relief to the surrounding hills and valleys. The summit is famous for a ruined tower built to commemorate the sixtieth anniversary of Queen Victoria's accession to the throne. It appears that a number of the spectators became very excited during the opening ceremony and the tower was partly demolished and has been left in this state ever since!

First published in 2005 by Myriad Books Limited 35 Bishopsthorpe Road, London SE26 4PA

Photographs copyright © Simon Kirwan     Text copyright © Myriad Books

Simon Kirwan has asserted his right under the Copyright, Designs and Patents Act 1998 to be identified as the author of this work.

ISBN 1 904736 09 2     Designed by Phillip Appleton     Printed in China     www.myriadbooks.com